Diego and Remy's
New Friendship
Authored & Illustrated By:
MARK DAROCHA

Diego is a boy with wavy brown hair, big brown eyes, and a smile that brightens everyone's day. He loves playing outside and going on aventuras (adventures) with his amigos (friends).

One sunny afternoon, Diego was playing with his favorite toy car when he heard a sound. "¡Guau, guau! Woof, woof! ¿Qué es? What could that be?" Diego wondered.

When Diego looked up, he saw a little brown-and-white puppy wagging its tail and gazing at him with eyes that were muy grande (very big). The puppy barked again, "¡Guau, guau! Woof, woof!"

Pero Diego wasn't sure if the puppy wanted to play or if it was lost. ¿Quién eres? ("Who are you?") Diego asked. "Where did you come from?"

Diego decided to say hola and slowly walked over to the puppy.

"Do you want to play?" Diego asked as he held out his toy car. The puppy sniffed it but no estaba interesada (was not interested). Diego sighed. "Maybe you don't like cars."

Diego thought for a moment, then ran inside to grab a pelota (ball). "How about this?" he asked, tossing the ball gently toward the puppy.

The puppy jumped up happily and chased the ball! "¡Sí!" Diego cheered. But just as Remy was about to bring the ball back, he stopped and looked at Diego with a little gimoteo (whine).

Diego *se sentó* (sat down) on the grass next to the puppy.

"¿Estás perdido? (Are you lost?)" Diego asked softly. He gave the puppy a gentle pat on the head. "You don't have to be scared. We can be *amigos* (friends)." The puppy wagged its tail and snuggled closer to Diego. "I think I'll call you Remy," Diego said with a big smile.

Now that Remy felt *seguro* (safe), he jumped up and barked happily. Diego threw the ball again, and this time, Remy brought it back, tail wagging *más rápido* (faster) than ever.

Diego laughed. "You just needed a little time, ¿verdad, Remy? (Right, Remy?) Now we're amigos!" And from then on, they played for hours.

Diego y (and) Remy had so much fun. Diego learned that sometimes making friends just takes paciencia (patience) and kindness.

And now, whenever they played together, Diego always remembered to say, "¡Buen trabajo, Remy! (Good job, Remy!) You're my best amigo (friend)!"

Now that Diego and Remy were friends, Remy would visit Diego every day!

"And whenever Remy barked, Diego would say, 'Let's play, Remy! ¡Guau, guau!' Woof, Woof!"

Diego and Remy were inseparable. They loved exploring and playing together.

"They played at the park," where Remy dashed after soccer balls and Diego laughed as he kicked them back. "¡Corre, Remy! (Run, Remy!)" Diego would call, clapping his hands as his pup sped across the field.

"They went to the beach!" The sound of waves and the warm sand made it their favorite getaway.

Diego built sandcastles with careful concentration while Remy dug happily beside him, wagging his tail. "¡Cuidado, Remy! (Careful, Remy!)" Diego laughed as Remy's tail knocked over the towers.

"And they even played after school!" Diego loved rushing home, dropping his backpack, and heading outside with his best amigo.

"Remy, ¿listo para jugar? (Ready to play?)" Diego asked, patting Remy's head. They raced across the yard, the sun casting warm golden light, as they laughed and played without a care in the world.

Diego y Remy wave goodbye, excited for their next aventura (adventure)!